Meet **Desert**
# ANIMALS

# KANGAROOS

## by Rose Davin

raintree
a Capstone company — publishers for children

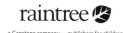

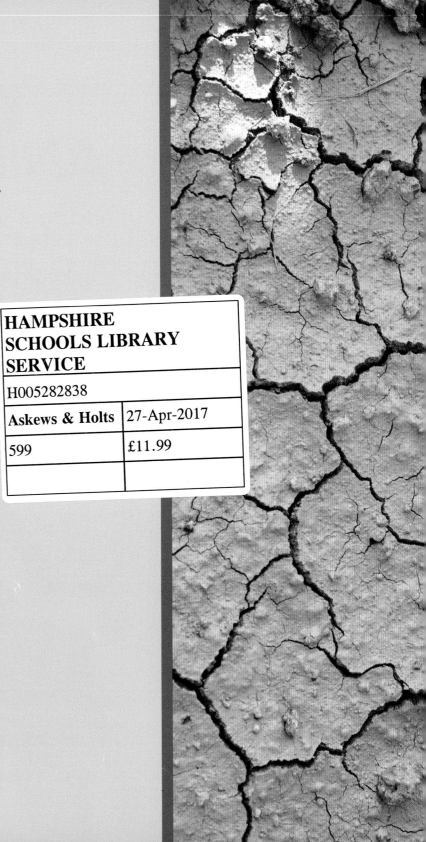

Raintree is an imprint of Capstone Global Library Limited, a company incorporated in England and Wales having its registered office at 264 Banbury Road, Oxford, OX2 7DY – Registered company number: 6695582

www.raintree.co.uk
myorders@raintree.co.uk

ISBN 978 1 4747 3660 2
20 19 18 17 16
10 9 8 7 6 5 4 3 2 1

British Library Cataloguing in Publication Data
A full catalogue record for this book is available from the British Library.

Editorial Credits
Marysa Storm and Alesha Sullivan, editors; Kayla Rossow, designer; Ruth Smith, media researcher; Kathy McColley, production specialist

Photo Credits
Ardea: © Jean-Paul Ferrero, 21; Capstone Press: 6; naturepl.com: Rolan Seitre, 15; Shutterstock: Christopher Meder, 1, Asian Images, 2, 24, Ilia Torlin, 7, John Carnemolla, cover, back cover, 5, K.A.Willis, 17, Karel Gallas, 13, Kjuuurs, 24, mark higgins, 9, optionm, 22, Rafael Ramirez Lee, 11, Warren Field, 19

## Note to Parents and Teachers

The Meet Desert Animals set supports national curriculum standards for science related to life science and ecosystems. This book describes and illustrates kangaroos. The images support early readers in understanding the text. The repetition of words and phrases helps early readers learn new words. This book also introduces early readers to subject-specific vocabulary words, which are defined in the Glossary section. Early readers may need assistance to read some words and to use the Table of Contents, Glossary, Read more, Websites, Comprehension questions and Index sections of the book.

Printed and bound in China.

# CONTENTS

# HIGH HOPPERS

Hop! A kangaroo jumps into the air.

It hops on its big hind feet.

A kangaroo's strong tail helps it

to move and stand.

Kangaroos live in Australia and
on nearby islands. They live in deserts,
woodlands and grasslands.
Some kangaroos live in groups called mobs.

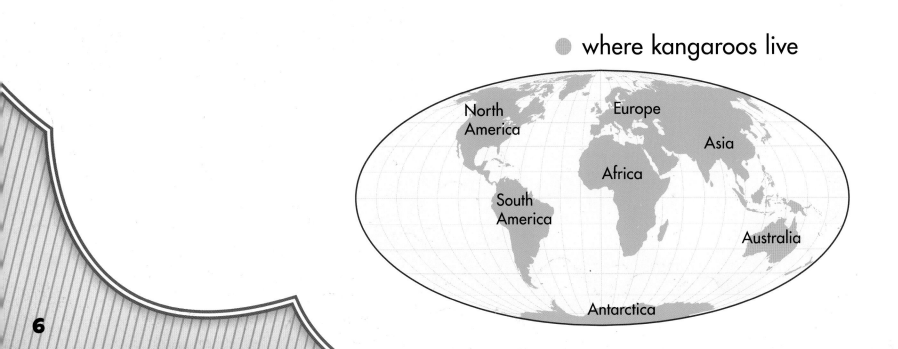

● where kangaroos live

North America

Europe

Asia

Africa

South America

Australia

Antarctica

# BIG AND SMALL

Some kangaroos are big. They weigh
about 91 kilograms (200 pounds).
Others are little. They weigh only
340 grams (12 ounces).

Kangaroos have brown, grey or red fur.

They have strong back legs with big feet.

Their front legs are short.

# TIME TO EAT

Kangaroos eat at night.

They munch on grass, leaves and shrubs.

# LIFE CYCLE

A female kangaroo usually has

one baby at a time.

Kangaroo babies are called joeys.

Newborn joeys are hairless.

They are about 2.5 centimetres (1 inch) long.

15

Joeys grow in their mothers' pouches.

They drink their mothers' milk.

Older joeys go in and out of the pouches.

Cluck! Kangaroo mothers call to their

joeys to keep them near.

Kangaroos listen for danger with their big ears.

They pound their feet on the ground.

This warns the mob of danger.

Wild dogs called dingoes attack kangaroos.
Kangaroos fight these predators with their
hind feet. Kangaroos can live about 8 years
in the wild.

21

# Glossary

**desert** area of dry land with few plants; deserts receive little rain

**grassland** open land covered mostly with grass

**island** piece of land that is surrounded by water

**mob** group of kangaroos that lives together; each mob has up to 20 kangaroos

**pouch** flap of skin that looks like a pocket in which some animals carry their young; young kangaroos live in the pouches after they are born

**predator** animal that hunts other animals for food

**woodland** land that is covered by trees and shrubs

# Read more

*From Joey to Kangaroo* (Start to Finish), Lisa Owings (Lerner Classroom, 2016)

*Kangaroos* (Seedlings), Kate Riggs (Creative Paperbacks, 2017)

*The Story of the Kangaroo* (Fabulous Animals), Anita Ganeri (Raintree, 2016)

# Websites

http://www.bbc.co.uk/nature/life/Red_Kangaroo
Learn all about the red kangaroo.

http://kids.nationalgeographic.com/animals/kangaroo/#kangaroo-hopping.jpg
Play games and watch videos of kangaroos on the National Geographic website.

# Comprehension questions

1. How do you think a pouch helps keep joeys safe?

2. Why are big ears helpful to a kangaroo?

3. In what ways are kangaroos social animals?
   How might this be helpful?

# Index